Cornwall's Far West

The Land's End peninsula in the far west of the county is an area of striking contrasts; a landscape of spectacular cliffs, golden beaches and twisting lanes. From **Hayle** (*right*), where the estuary of the River Hayle opens out into the broad sweep of St. Ives Bay, several miles of sandy beaches and sand dunes can be reached. At Godrevy Point a dangerous channel between the mainland and tiny Godrevy Island claimed many victims until a lighthouse was built in 1859 to warn sailors away from the savage rocks.

Nearby **Carbis Bay** (*left*) enjoys a mild climate and its sheltered, sandy beach lies beneath a steep hillside to which houses and hotels cling. There are excellent cliff walks here and the nearby rocks are a popular spot for fishermen. **St. Ives** (*middle and below*) was once one of Cornwall's most prosperous ports and the harbour is still a busy centre of activity in the town. Artists have been attracted here since the 19th century and the presence of a vibrant artistic community has done much to preserve the character of this ancient fishing port. This is also a popular area with summer visitors who enjoy the mild climate and the fine sandy beaches of St. Ives Bay.

A lighthouse has stood on the rocky headland at **Pendeen Watch** (*above*) for more than one hundred years, guiding shipping round the dangerous coast to the north of Cape Cornwall. The village of Sennen is the most westerly community of mainland Britain and nearby **Sennen Cove** (*right*), with its beaches and narrow quay, stands at one end of the magnificent sweep of Whitesand Bay. The tiny harbour is sheltered below steep slopes, and here is housed the lifeboat which is nearest to wild Land's End, England's most westerly point. The spectacular, 200-feet-high granite cliffs at **Land's End** (*below*) are constantly battered by Atlantic waves and gales which have created bizarre rock forms offshore. Standing more than a mile out to sea, the Longships Lighthouse warns shipping away from this treacherous stretch of the coast.

The tiny village of **Porthcurno** is situated on the wild and rocky Penwith peninsula some three miles from Land's End. Here a beautiful little cove (*right*) of almost white sand is sheltered by jagged granite headlands which take the force of the constant battering by the winds and waves breaking over offshore rocks.

Seen here from Raginnis Hill, which leads steeply out of the village to the west, picturesque **Mousehole** (*left*) has a long and fascinating history. Many quaint, stone-built cottages cluster in the narrow streets and alleyways around its snug little harbour. It was here that Dolly Pentreath died in 1777, the last person known to use the Cornish language as her native tongue. Mousehole was Cornwall's main fishing port for many years and although it lost trade in the 19th century to Newlyn, some two miles to the north, it still provides welcome shelter for small craft. Despite the difficulties facing the modern fishing industry, **Newlyn** (*below*) remains the main fishing port in the south-west. The lively quayside is always busy and a large fish market is held here. Fishing boats and leisure craft invariably create a colourful scene in the horseshoe-shaped harbour. An artists' colony was established here in 1883 and Newlyn is still famous as a centre for artists.

Superbly situated on the wide sweep of Mount's Bay, **Penzance** (*above*) is England's most westerly town. Once it was a major West Country port and the harbour is still a bustling centre of activity. Mainly used by private craft, it is also the point from which the ferry plies between the mainland and the Isles of Scilly. Connected to the mainland by a stone causeway which is only accessible at low tide, the rocky pyramid of **St. Michael's Mount** (*top right*) rises nearly 300 feet from the waters of Mount's Bay. It was originally the site of a Benedictine priory established by Edward the Confessor, but is now topped by a spectacular 14th century castle. A popular holiday village, **Praa Sands** (*bottom right*) overlooks a sandy beach backed by dunes and

sheltered from the westerly winds by high cliffs. Once an important seaport, **Porthleven** (*below*) has a large harbour enclosed between steep banks and protected from westerly storms by a breakwater and an outer harbour. The inner harbour and wharf date from the 19th century when they were built for exporting tin and copper and importing machinery, but today they provide a safe haven for sailors along this treacherous section of the coast.

The Lizard

Most southerly point of England, the Lizard peninsula is known for its rugged rocks and delightful sandy coves. **Mullion Cove** (*above*), with its small harbour, is about a mile from the pretty little village of Mullion. Facing west across wide Mount's Bay, the cove is exposed to the full fury of the Atlantic, and the harbour was built in 1839 following a severe storm which destroyed many of Mullion's fishing boats.

Some of the most spectacular scenery on the entire Lizard peninsula is to be found near **Kynance Cove** (*above*). Here the sea has carved numerous caves and arches in the cliffs which are veined with the purples, reds and greens of the remarkable serpentine rock. At high tide the swirling sea rushes with dramatic effect through gaps in the rock. At **Lizard Point** (*left*) the cliffs reach a height of 180 feet offering splendid views of this dramatic stretch of coast. Cornwall's first lighthouse was built on the point in 1619 and its successor, constructed in 1751, throws its light a distance of 29 nautical miles.

Known for its rocky coastline and delightful sandy coves, the Lizard peninsula is the most southerly point of England. At **Kennack Sands** (*right*) two beaches are joined together at low tide making one of the longest stretches of sand on the eastern side of the peninsula. Lying at the foot of a steep and heavily wooded valley between rocky headlands, **Cadgwith** (*below*) is one of the most picturesque coves in the county where crab and lobster boats are drawn up on the little shingle beach when they are not at sea.

Among the other picturesque fishing villages on the Lizard are **Porthallow** (*left*), with its wide beach backed by steep, wooded hills, and **Coverack** (*below*). Here the minute harbour has for centuries provided a refuge for fishermen on this exposed stretch of coast with its dangerous offshore rocks.

Falmouth and Roseland

Now a popular holiday centre, situated on a superb bay, **Falmouth** (*top and middle*) has been a flourishing port for more than 200 years and has one of the finest natural harbours in the world. Located on the harbour waterfront, the National Maritime Museum Cornwall (*top*) is the centrepiece of an international leisure complex. The museum itself comprises a number of galleries with displays on themes relating to boats and the sea including the stories of some famous craft, navigation and meteorology, boat building and the Cornish maritime heritage. Often regarded as the gateway to the Lizard peninsula, the ancient market town of **Helston** (*bottom right*) received its first charter from King John in 1201. The handsome Victorian Guildhall stands imposingly in the centre of the town. Helston is best known today for the famous annual Furry Dance which takes place in May to celebrate the coming of summer. From Helston it is a short distance to the superb pastoral scenery of the **Helford River**, a tranquil haven of narrow creeks and well-wooded banks. Helford Passage (*bottom left*) is a popular anchorage for small craft, its sand and shingle beach facing south across the estuary.

The beautiful and unspoilt Roseland peninsula includes the dignified little resort of St. Mawes as well as a number of picturesque villages. One of Cornwall's many diminutive ports and harbours, the delightful little fishing village of **Portloe** (*left*) nestles in a steep valley and its slipway is still well used by local fishermen. **Portscatho** (*top right*), with its narrow streets and tiny harbour, was once a quiet fishing village, but the boats which crowd into the harbour today are mainly used for pleasure. Legend has it that the unusual round houses at **Veryan** (*top left*), their thatched roofs surmounted by a cross, were built in the Regency period for the five daughters of the vicar. The shape was intended to eliminate corners in which the devil could hide. **St. Mawes** (*bottom*), with its sheltered harbour and small sandy beaches, is a popular centre for boating activities of all kinds. Built up in terraces and well protected both from the north and the south, St. Mawes shares the mild climate which has justly earned this part of the coast the title of 'Cornish Riviera'.

Surrounded by scenery of the utmost beauty, the River Fal flows between wooded banks with countless delightful creeks leading off to right and left. Set on one of the most beautiful stretches of the river, the **King Harry Ferry** (*right*) is named after Henry VI who swam the river here on horseback.

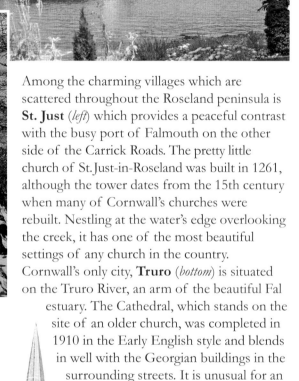

Among the charming villages which are scattered throughout the Roseland peninsula is **St. Just** (*left*) which provides a peaceful contrast with the busy port of Falmouth on the other side of the Carrick Roads. The pretty little church of St. Just-in-Roseland was built in 1261, although the tower dates from the 15th century when many of Cornwall's churches were rebuilt. Nestling at the water's edge overlooking the creek, it has one of the most beautiful settings of any church in the country.

Cornwall's only city, **Truro** (*bottom*) is situated on the Truro River, an arm of the beautiful Fal estuary. The Cathedral, which stands on the site of an older church, was completed in 1910 in the Early English style and blends in well with the Georgian buildings in the surrounding streets. It is unusual for an English church in that all three towers are crowned by stone spires.

Newquay and the Atlantic Coast

Many of Cornwall's former mining centres have now become pleasant little resorts. **Portreath** (*below*) was once a thriving mining centre, and the eight-mile-long tramroad that linked the port to mines near Redruth has now been turned into a waymarked walk and cycle track. Vast quantities of coal and copper ore were shipped from the little harbour and the incline where wagons were lowered from the tramroad can still be seen.

Rowing boats are now drawn up on to the beach in Trevaunance Cove at **St. Agnes** (*right*) where tin and copper were once shipped from the tiny harbour using a system of pulleys, winches and chutes. The wild, rocky ridge of **Carn Brea** (*below*) which is believed to have been the site of a Neolithic camp, overlooks Redruth. Rising to 740 feet, it offers splendid views and is crowned by the remains of a castle occupied in the 15th century by local landowners.

Beautifully situated on the southern side of the sandy Gannel estuary is the pretty village of **Crantock** (*right*). As well as the charming, thatched Old Albion Inn, Crantock has many attractive colour-washed, stone cottages which cluster around a tiny square. Just south of Crantock, **Holywell Bay** (*below*) has a large sandy beach which is popular with surfers.

Perranporth (*below*) is known for its magnificent stretch of firm sand which extends for more than two miles. It takes its name from St. Piran who is said to have sailed from Ireland on a millstone to establish his first church here. He became the patron saint of the Cornish people who celebrate St. Piran's Day on March 5th.

Although it is Cornwall's largest holiday resort and Britain's main surfing centre, **Newquay** (*right and below*), is an ancient town and the 'new quay' from which it takes its name probably dates from the 15th century. Visitors are attracted by the sheltered bays and sandy beaches, many of which are reached by steps and ramps cut into the cliffs. Despite its popularity as a modern resort, Newquay retains much of its character as an old fishing and trading port and the harbour, which dries out at low tide to provide another beach, is well used by small boats. North of the town are **Bedruthan Steps** (*top*), one of many outstanding beauty spots which face the open Atlantic on this memorable stretch of coast. These detached offshore rocks were created by the action of the sea, but legend has it that they were the stepping stones of the Cornish giant, Bedruthan.

Around Padstow

With its picturesque harbour and bustling quayside, **Padstow** (*below*) stands on the western side of the broad estuary of the River Camel. This ancient little fishing port is the gateway to some of Cornwall's loveliest bays including **Trevone** (*below right*) where the delightful little sandy bay is sheltered by low cliffs. Some five miles to the west of Padstow, the rocky promontory of **Trevose Head** (*centre*) thrusts out into the Atlantic surmounted by a lighthouse which was first erected in 1847.

Among the many delightful little sandy bays which lie in the shelter of Trevose Head is horseshoe-shaped **Harlyn Bay** (*bottom left*). One of the most important collections of prehistoric remains ever made in Britain was found at Harlyn in 1900 when an Iron Age cemetery was discovered here.

Either side of rugged Trevose Head there are several delightful little bays with sandy beaches washed by Atlantic rollers, making this stretch of the coast a favourite area with surfers. Behind the beach at **Constantine Bay** (*top*), the dunes are planted with marram grass to hold up the process of erosion which poses a constant threat for this coastline.

At nearby **Treyarnon Bay** (*above*) a little stream winds across the beach from the low cliffs behind it and sandy **Porthcothan Bay** (*left*) is cradled between rocky headlands which offer some fine rock scenery. **Mother Ivey's Bay** (*below*), situated on the sheltered eastern side of Trevose Head, is properly known as Polventon Bay, but it acquired its more usual name from an old woman who claimed the wreckage which was washed ashore here.

Situated at the head of an inlet at the mouth of the Camel estuary, the little resort of **Polzeath** (*top*) has a superb expanse of sand enclosed by rocks and sheltered by nearby Pentire Point. Situated about a mile to the south at **Trebetherick** (*right*), the ancient Church of St. Enodoc overlooks **Daymer Bay** (*below right*) where the sandy beach is framed by low cliffs. The church was at one time almost entirely engulfed by sand but was later reclaimed and restored. Sir John Betjeman, a former Poet Laureate, lived near here and

is buried in the churchyard. **Rock** (*below left*) is the main centre for sailing and water-skiing on the River Camel and the wide, sandy beach is always crowded with colourful yachts and dinghies. The village has been linked by ferry with Padstow, on the other side of the river, since the 14th century and there are some pleasant walks northwards along the cliffs overlooking the estuary.

North Cornwall

In the 19th century, **Port Gaverne** (*below*) was a busy pilchard-fishing port which also handled slate, coal and limestone, and engaged in shipbuilding. Situated at the head of a sheltered inlet on the beautiful North Cornwall Heritage Coast, it is today a peaceful hamlet with ancient cottages crowded into narrow streets on the hillside above the cove. A few fishing boats are still drawn up on the safe little beach when they are not at sea, and a fish market is held on the quayside.

Trebarwith (*right*) is enclosed between steep hillsides at the northern end of Port Isaac Bay. Sailing ships once called here to trade Welsh coal for slate which had to be hauled down the cliffs to the boats waiting below. Offshore the bulk of Gull Rock dominates the view seawards.

The tiny haven of **Port Isaac** (*left*) is undoubtedly one of the most picturesque of Cornwall's many fishing villages. Here ancient cottages cling to the precipitous slopes above the harbour. An extensive fleet once fished out of Port Isaac and the little harbour still provides a welcome haven for fishermen along this rugged coast.

Between the high moors and the
stormy seas of this treacherous and
rocky coast lies the village of **Boscastle**
(*right*) with its sturdy cottages clinging to
the hillside. The tiny River Valency
winds through the sheltered valley to
the narrow, rock-enclosed harbour
which was once busy with sailing ships
loading slate from the local mines.
Now it provides one of the few refuges
from the stormy seas which batter the
rugged North Cornwall coast.

Tintagel is traditionally associated with
the stories of King Arthur and his Knights
of the Round Table. Perched on the cliffs
300 feet above the sea in an area of breath-
taking scenic beauty, Tintagel Castle (*left*)
was the legendary birthplace of King
Arthur. Although the present ruins date
only from about 1145, the remains of an
ancient Celtic monastery nearby support
the theory that the castle was built on the
site of an earlier palace which existed in
the Dark Ages. The quaint Old Post Office
(*below*), situated in Tintagel's main street, is
built in the style of a medieval manor
house and dates from the 14th century.

With its little sand and shingle beach, **Crackington Haven** (*top*) lies between the towering cliffs of Pencannow Point to the north and Cambeak in the south. Much of the coast near this romantic spot is owned and protected by The National Trust and cliff-top walks offer some magnificent views of the spectacular coastal scenery. The most northerly town in Cornwall, the popular resort of **Bude** is surrounded by dramatic cliff scenery and makes an excellent centre from which to explore the local countryside. The area was once notorious for the wreckers who looted the many ships which came to grief on this treacherous rocky coast. Now Bude is famous for its extensive sands and

surf which are known to surfers from all over the world. To the south nothing impedes the relentless surge of the Atlantic rollers into Widemouth Bay (*above*) while Bude's other superb beaches are favourites with holiday-makers. At Summerleaze Beach (*left*), the most central of the town's beaches, there is a wide expanse of firm sand backed by grassy downland. A large swimming pool on the beach is filled each day by the tides.

Around Bodmin Moor

A landscape of contrasts, Bodmin Moor is designated an Area of Outstanding Natural Beauty, and attracts both naturalists and ramblers with its wild and rugged beauty. The attractive small town of **Bodmin** (*below*) lies on the south-western fringes of the moor and makes an excellent centre for exploring the surrounding area. Overlooking the River Fowey to the south-east of Bodmin, **Lanhydrock** (*right*) is one of the most outstanding of Cornwall's many superb gardens. The formal gardens, with their lawns and flower-beds, date from 1857 and near the gatehouse stands a group of neat, clipped yew trees.

Standing in lonely isolation on bleak moorland, often shrouded in mist, **Jamaica Inn** (*below*) at Bolventor is redolent with the atmosphere of the 18th century when it was a staging post on the Bodmin to Launceston road for the London mail coach. It is said that smugglers used to store their contraband at the inn which gained enduring fame when Daphne du Maurier used it as the setting for her novel of the same name. Less than two miles away, high on the moor, is Dozmary Pool where legend has it that King Arthur's sword Excalibur was returned to the mysterious Lady of the Lake.

The timeless and mysterious atmosphere which pervades lonely Bodmin is emphasised by the presence of numerous awe-inspiring anancient monuments. Spectacular **Trethevy Quoit** (*below*) is an outstanding example of a chieftain's tomb which dates from Neolithic times. The massive capstone weighs around ten and a half tons. The granite ridge of **Rough Tor** (*top*) rises up on the western side of the moor.

Dominating the surrounding countryside from its position on a mound, **Launceston Castle** (*above*) was built in Norman times to guard the main route from Devon into Cornwall. The original wooden fort later became a formidable fortress which was fiercely contested during the Civil War before it finally fell to Cromwell's forces in 1646.

Cornish Riviera

With its mild climate and profusion of subtropical trees and shrubs, Cornwall's southern coast has earned the title of 'Cornish Riviera'. One of a number of picturesque little fishing ports and resorts, **Mevagissey** (*left*) is always noisy with the cries of gulls, and the inner and outer harbours are busy with fishing boats, yachts and other colourful small craft. To the south is **Gorran Haven** (*below right*), a popular resort with a sheltered, sandy beach and a little stone quay which is well used by fishermen. Dating from the early 17th century, the **Lost Gardens of Heligan** (*below left*) near Mevagissey lay forgotten for over 70 years. They have now been returned to their former splendour in one of Europe's largest garden restoration projects.

Close to **St. Austell** (*middle right*), a centre of the china clay industry, there are a number of little ports which became important outlets for the trade. **Charlestown** (*left*), designed by John Smeaton, is a perfect example of a small-scale 18th century port. Facing onto St. Austell Bay, **Polkerris** (*middle left*) is a secluded little cove with a sandy beach sheltered by an old stone jetty. In Tudor times it was a centre for the pilchard industry and the old cellars where the fish were processed can still be seen. Situated in an old clay pit, the **Eden Project** (*bottom*) demonstrates the fascinating story of man's relationship with plants. It covers an area of 125 acres, housing 4,000 species from tropical to temperate zones in giant geodesic domes.

Fowey and Polruan face each other across the busy estuary of the River Fowey. With its network of narrow streets climbing steeply up from the harbour, **Fowey** (*left*) has been a busy port since the Middle Ages and is one of the most attractive of Cornwall's ancient coastal towns. The harbour provides safe anchorage for hundreds of yachts and the quay is always a busy and colourful scene of activity. Linked to Fowey by a passenger ferry, the ancient little port of **Polruan** (*below*) was once a busy shipbuilding village.

Bodinnick (*bottom*) is a typically Cornish hamlet where quaint old cottages line a breakneck hill as it descends to the ferry slip. Beside the slipway stands *Ferryside*, the house where novelist Daphne du Maurier did much of her writing. A car ferry plies across the deep estuary from Bodinnick to the busy port of Fowey. From above the village, there are superb views towards Gribbin Head and distant Dodman Point.

Once the capital of Cornwall, the picturesque old town of **Lostwithiel** stands in a thickly-wooded valley and has many ancient buildings. A fine medieval bridge spans the River Fowey which is renowned among anglers for its salmon and trout. Nearby, perched on a high mound within a moat, stand the ruins of **Restormel Castle** (*left*). Built during Norman times, it is Cornwall's best-preserved military building and the huge circular keep was garrisoned during the Civil War.

Several miles upstream from Fowey the river divides into two. The wider branch continues north-west towards Lostwithiel while the beautiful **Lerryn River** (*right*) flows north-east passing, on its way the charming old village of Lerryn. Winding past thickly wooded banks and frequented by heron and curlew, this little stream is without doubt one of the most delightful and attractive parts of the lovely Fowey estuary.

Situated at the foot of a deep wooded combe amid rugged coastal scenery, **Polperro** (*above and right*) is one of England's most attractive and enchanting fishing villages. Old white-washed cottages cluster around the tiny, bustling harbour which was once famous as a centre for smuggling, but which now provides a safe haven for both fishing boats and pleasure craft.

Remote **Talland Bay** (*left*) has been the setting for many shipwrecks in years gone by and in the 18th and 19th centuries it became a notorious base for smugglers. From the little beach of sand, shingle and rock, steep paths lead up to the headland where the Cornwall South Coast Path offers some fine views of the impressive coastal scenery.

Sandwiched between precipitous hills and rugged cliffs, the ancient towns of **East** and **West Looe** face each other across the busy harbour. This is a popular centre for both fishermen and holiday-makers, and the sandy beach is sheltered by a jetty known as Banjo Pier because of its unusual shape. Also popular with visitors, the little village of **Downderry** (*below inset*) has a beach of silvery sand and shingle and is a good centre for angling and walking. Just over two miles from Looe, **Seaton** (*below*) has an attractive sandy beach sheltered by tree-covered cliffs.

Whitsand Bay (*right*) is deceptively peaceful on a calm day but this four-mile-long stretch of coast can be treacherous in rough weather when the strong south-westerly winds whip the surf into a frenzy. In the days of sail it was a graveyard for many ships as they struggled to reach the shelter of Plymouth Sound. The strong cross-currents still make the sea dangerous for swimmers, but the fine sandy beach can be reached by paths which zigzag down the cliffs.

The neighbouring villages of **Cawsand** (*top left*) and **Kingsand** (*bottom left*) lie on the Rame peninsula and at one time were divided by the county boundary with Kingsand being in Devon. Now both are in Cornwall. They look out across Cawsand Bay which was an important anchorage before Plymouth's breakwater was built. In 1815 Napoleon was anchored here on the warship which was carrying him to exile on St. Helena after his defeat at Waterloo. Today they are peaceful little villages with narrow streets, pretty colour-washed buildings and little sand-and-shingle beaches sheltered from the prevailing winds by Rame.